—Youth Edition—

A Bishop Called
Bonnie

The Hines Sisters

A Bishop Called Bonnie

Copyright © 2024 The Hines Sisters

All rights reserved. No part of this publication may be reproduced, stored in any retrieval system, or transmitted in any form or by any means, mechanical, photocopying, recording, or otherwise, without permission in writing from the publisher, except by a reviewer, who may quote brief passages in a review.

Cover and Interior design by Ted Ruybal
Contributions by Kirsten Martin
100% Human Made. No AI used.

Manufactured in the United States of America

Wisdom House Books
For more information, please contact:
www.wisdomhousebooks.com

Hardback ISBN: 979-8-9906787-0-5
LCCN: 2024941553

REL000000 | RELIGION / General
BIO018000 | BIOGRAPHY & AUTOBIOGRAPHY / Religious
YAN047000 | YOUNG ADULT NONFICTION / Religion / General

1 2 3 4 5 6 7 8 9 10

A Bishop Called
Bonnie

The Hines Sisters

*Renita J. Hines, Marcia Hines Parrish,
Charlotte Hines Wallace*

*Foreword by
Bishop George E. Battle, Jr.*

*Epilogue by
Bishop Darryl B. Starnes, Sr.*

Circle of Love

B onnie's Secret to Success was found in the "God-Fearing" committed Women of Zion . . . They surrounded her with a circle of love and unconditional support!

To God Be the Glory!

In Their Own Words

The words "I love you more . . ." ring in our ears and resonate in our hearts. How often did we hear our dear sister, Bishop Mildred Bonnie Hines, speak these words? The words, "I love you more" represented the belief from which she lived her life.

God spoke to His people and declared in 1 Corinthians 13:13 ESV . . . "so now faith, hope and love abide, these three; but the greatest of these is love." Apostle Paul, author of 1 Corinthians had a primary message to the people from Jesus. Jesus wanted the readers to know that His followers were held to a standard of integrity and morality as they sought to represent Jesus' ways of life.

'Bishop' as we fondly called her, held the utmost faith in the word of Jesus and wanted everyone to value living a life full of love. She accepted the Word of God as being true, genuine, and, therefore, real. Henceforth, every individual she touched was the recipient of the gift of love, as she preached the importance of love and exemplified the beauty of love in our lives. Her life was a textbook example on integrity and morality.

We recognize how blessed we were to have 'The Bishop' as our sister. She was an amazing servant of God whose loving teachings and examples of living a life full of love will not be forgotten. Our lives have been dearly enriched by knowing and loving her. We cherish her memory and realize that so many colleagues, dear family members and friends miss her.

This publication is humbly dedicated to the memory of our dear sister and is a labor of love by many. We have collaborated with her distinguished colleagues, family, and friends to share the loving actions of Bishop Mildred Bonnie Hines, during her life on earth. To God Be the Glory!

As we begin to share this journey through A Bishop Called Bonnie, we want to offer our deepest appreciation to Bishop Walker for his guidance and support as Senior Bishop in the early stages of her campaign. It was with his wise council that she was able to navigate successfully through the election process.

However, it was toward the end of her service that Bishop Warren Brown stepped in to hold up her arms in carrying on the work. As a retired Bishop, his years of experience served as a blessing and gave strength to her leadership in the South Atlantic Episcopal Area.

In addition, we want to pause to applaud the South Atlantic members for their outstanding contribution to the success of the district. The Bishop called them "Team Hines." They supported her unconditionally with love, dedication, and creativity. So much so that the distance from the South Atlantic Area to California became just a "Zoom" call away. Praise God for technology!!!

Love to all,
The Hines Sisters

In Memory

༄

In Memory of Mama and Daddy

Train up a child in the way he should go; and when he is old, he will not depart from it.

—Proverbs 22:6 (KJV)

Never Forget Maria, "Baby Sister."

So now faith, hope, and, love abide, these three, but the greatest of these is love.

—1 Corinthians 13:13 (ESV)

Dedication

THIS BOOK IS DEDICATED TO THE CHILDREN OF ZION.

Lest they never forget her
history-changing contribution
to the AME Zion Church.

Table of Contents

Foreword xix
Introduction xxiii
Childhood and Family 1
   In the Beginning 3
   Growing Up 5
   "I Discipline My Students with Hugs" 6
   Grandma's House 8
   Church and More Church 10
   The Bell Ringer 11
   Caring for Others 12
The Change in Life 13
   The Sound of Music 15
From Worship to Work 17
   "From Worship to Work" 19
   Belk Teen Board 20
Leadership 23
   The Pastor 25
   The Invitation 29
   Leadership 31
   Teamwork Makes the Dreamwork 32
   Service 35
   An Election We Will Never Forget 36
   First Female Elected in 226 Years 38
   The Assignment 39
   A Very Special Blessing 40
   Africa . . . Another World 41
   The Lighthouse 43

Table of Contents (Cont.)

A Leap of Faith 45
   To God Be the Glory. 47
   A Life of Service 48
   Footprints Around the World. 49
   A New Home: The House that Bonnie Built. 50
   Reflections . . . In Their own Words 51

Living with Great Expectations 53
   Bishop Kenneth Monroe, African Methodist Episcopal Zion Church

A Tribute to Bishop Mildred "Bonnie" Hines 57
   Rev. Dr. Dwight cannon, Executive Director of Global Missions and Editor in Chief the Missionary *Seer*

Reflections on Bishop Mildred Bonnie Hines 61
   Bishop Warren M. Brown

Tribute to the Right Reverend Mildred "Bonnie" Hines, 1955-2022 65
   Lovetta J. Holmes, Missionary Supervisor

A Tribute to My Childhood Frend . . . Bishop Mildred Bonnie Hines . . 69
   Amy M. White

A Tribute to My Friend and My Leader 73
   Rev. Dr. Valerie A Maness

Her Mentors and Mothers 77
   Joann B Holmes and Glenda H. Manning

Honoring Bishop Mildred B. Hines Author Reverend Jerred McDaniel, Senior Pastor, First A.M.E. Zion Church, Pasadena, California 80

Who Was Bishop Mildred "Bonnie" Hines? 81
   The Etymology of Right Reverend Mildred "Bonnie" Hines. 82
   Rev. Dr. Sheldon Shipman
   What You May or May Not Know About Bonnie 83

Table of Contents (cont.)

Official Documents 85
   Education, Work, Church and Civic Service 86
   Resolution of Comfort on the Service of Triumph for the Right Reverend Mildred "Bonnie" Hines, Greenville Memorial AME Church 89
   Obituary 92
   Order of Service 95
With Thanks 97
   Acknowledgements 98
   Glossary of Terms 101
Epilogue "First" 107
   Bishop Darryl B. Starnes, Sr., Senior Bishop of the African Methodist Episcopal Zion Church
Photo Gallery 111
Thank You 129

Foreword

Bishop George E. Battle, Jr.
(84th in the line of Succession)
Retired Senior Bishop of The
African Methodist Episcopal Zion Church

Sometimes a brief conversation can change the whole course of your life. It may begin casually with a nod or a smile to someone you sit down beside or serve with as a pastor. However, years later, you are sharing as colleagues on the Board of Bishops for The African Methodist Episcopal Zion Church.

When Bishop Mildred Bernetta "Bonnie" Hines' family and friends called and asked me to consider writing the foreword to A Bishop Called Bonnie, I immediately felt a deep sense of honor. For one thing, I have spent time with Bonnie over the years to be blessed by her life, her powerful biblical preaching and teaching, and her real friendship. She has preached for me during the conferences that I presided over and was the teacher for many sessions during the Leadership Training in the Episcopal Districts that I served. Her long ministry in Charlotte, North Carolina and Los Angeles, California, leaves little doubt that the hand of the Lord was on this woman.

I can understand why the thunderous applaud happened in 2008 when Bishop Mildred "Bonnie" Hines was elected as the first female bishop and the 98th in the line of succession in The African Methodist Episcopal Zion Church. One of my fondest memories will always be when Bonnie and I would visit on the phone and have the best time of fellowship during her first years in that position. It was a time filled with conversation, memories, scripture reading, prayer, and encouragement.

I am also honored to write this because of my own profound love for Bishop Mildred "Bonnie" Hines. The impact of her life and testimony on my own life and ministry can never be overstated. The first time I actually saw Bonnie facilitate a workshop at one of the connectional meetings, I had a question I wanted to ask her. I wanted to know what she thought about being filled with the Holy Spirit and having the ability to share this knowledge with so many. I have never forgotten my first encounter and conversation with her. When she had finished, she simply waited to hear a response from me, then the conversation continued. She treated me so graciously.

I will always remember when she came to the New

England Conference to serve as the Associate Bishop. Here, she shared the love of God from the pulpit. During her introduction, she would sometimes say, "Now, my beloved, as I preach from God's Word today, you may hear some things from me that you have all heard from Bishop Battle." Of course, she was being funny, and the audience roared with laughter!

You will read similar stories about Bishop Hines in this book, A Bishop Called Bonnie. Her sisters, Renita J. Hines, Marcia Hines Parrish, Charlotte Hines Wallace, and their friend, Glenda Horton Manning compiled this book to provide insight most people may not have ever heard of the Bonnie we did not fully know. It is unique, and I am really excited and delighted that the family and friends have taken the time to add yet another dimension to Bishop Mildred "Bonnie" Hines' wonderful testimony for the Lord, Jesus the Christ.

Introduction

Grace and peace be with you as you go on a brief journey to know Bishop Bonnie better.

A *Bishop Called Bonnie* is dedicated to and written for the children of Zion. It is the desire of her sisters that you meet this Brave soul and lover of our Lord and Savior Jesus Christ. Her sisters were present in every age and stage of her life. They counted it a privilege to support her as she tried to fulfill God's plan for her life.

She was special in that she was raised by her mother and father with four sisters in a God-fearing home. She was unique in that she always wanted to be a preacher, even as a little child. However, she was miraculous in that she was elected to the bishopric as she broke the "glass ceiling" of the church on her way to Glory. She Made History!

She was the first female to be elected to the highest post in the history of our world church. And to the writing of this book, history must record that she was the only woman to serve on the Board of Bishops, presiding as President for a six-month term.

Praise God for her gifts and willingness to serve. And so, for you, children of Zion, it can happen again! There is a place in this great big church for you to serve if you desire, and are willing to go where no one else has ever gone and do what no one else has ever done for the "up-building" of God's kingdom.

Bonnie was a trailblazer who laid a clear path for others to follow. This book is being published because many loving, talented women said, "yes." They said "yes" to the calls, emails, and text messages. They said "yes" to the writing, editing and typing. They also offered wonderful words of encouragement and support.

Thank you to each and all of them!

As you read, you will find a short story recalled by each sister.

They want you to know and appreciate Bonnie as they did. Enjoy!

To God be the Glory!

Childhood & Family

The Lord is my shepherd . . .

—Psalm 23:1

Psalm 23

1. The Lord is my Shepherd

4. Even though I walk thru the Valley of the Shadow of death I will feel no evil for though art with me

6. Surely goodness and mercy shall follow me all the days of my life and I will dwell in the house of of the Lord for ever

—Bishop's handwriting—

In the Beginning

Mildred Bernadatta "Bonnie" Hines was born on May 6, 1955. She grew up in the beautiful countryside of Mount Airy, North Carolina.

She and her four sisters were raised by their parents JoAnn Gwyn Hines and Roscoe Hines.

They were taught to work together as a team, always looking out for each other and always sticking together. Bonnie was the leader, the oldest, Mama's "Big Girl."

Their home was a classroom. It was there that they learned excellent housekeeping skills. Most importantly, they learned that honesty and humility are what develop character

Mount Airy was named an All-American City in 1994. It is known as the birth place of actor Andy Griffith and inspired the fictional town of "Mayberry," North Carolina.

However, we want the history to show that Mount Airy is the little town in Surry County where Bishop Bonnie was born. Here is where she grew up, thrived, and overcame the trials of segregation. She rose to become the first female to reach the highest post of bishop of the AME Zion World Church.

We want her name to be listed among the notables in her hometown and the world.

Bonnie's house was like one long, never-ending "sleepover." All girls, all the time!

They shared everything . . . clothes, food, joy, and sadness.

Their parents maintained a God-fearing home, where worship through Bible reading, praying and singing always took place. At church, Bonnie and her sisters often blended their voices to sing to the glory of God. They were the "back up" for the lead singers, Mother JoAnne and Aunt Clarestine Gwyn Fulton, accompanied by the musical talents of Uncle Samuel Gwyn on organ and our great aunt, Kathleen Edmonds on piano.

*Mount Airy is a little town near Winston-Salem, in Surry County, North Carolina. Population: Approx. 10,388

Growing Up

Bonnie loved school and often spoke of her first-grade teacher Miss Virginia Galloway.

In that classroom, she developed a thirst for learning and a passion for public speaking. She loved English, Chemistry, History and Economics. Bonnie was a natural leader . . . full of courage and adventure.

Bonnie loved to climb the water pipes that ran through the city of Mt. Airy. She would gather her sisters and other neighborhood children, line them up by age, and make sure they saw that she would keep them safe until they got to the other side. She would cheer them on and then celebrate their success. She was a born "cheerleader" for others.

"I discipline my students with hugs."

Katherine Virginia Galloway, the first grade teacher for Bishop Mildred Bonnie Hines showered the Bishop with hugs and precious moments of inspiration. Everyone called this phenomenal teacher Miss Galloway and admired her immensely for each student was recognized as the child Miss Galloway never birthed. Bishop Hines repeatedly announced that as a young first grader Miss Galloway instilled in her a thirst for learning and a passion for speaking. So magnificent was the influence from Miss Galloway that Bonnie developed a love for English, Chemistry, History, and Home Economics while attending North Surry High School. She matriculated to Mars Hill College in Mars Hill, North Carolina having received an academic and athletic scholarship. The rest is history for the magnificence of this wonderful creature from God. I too was a student of Miss Galloway and wish to share with you the secret to the success of Miss Galloway's students. One can help but wonder in amazement what this petite lady, who often had to look up to her taller students to talk, used as such a powerful tool to make the students want to learn.

Miss Galloway could have written a book on the holistic approach to life and could have aided Hiliary Clinton in being an advocate for the belief that 'It takes a Village.' Throughout the day, every aspect of the actions of the students were guided by Miss Galloway. She never sat down in the classroom; she was always attentive to the students and encouraged the students to look at her rather than staring off.

I am certain that Mrs Hines got a report on Bonnie each Sunday when Miss Galloway went to St Paul AME Church where the two mothers and Bonnie attended church. Bishop Hines and I adored Miss Galloway as our Girl Scout Troop leader. Our troop was of course, the neatest and most industrious troop.

When the schools became integrated, Miss Galloway became the first black teacher to teach the first grade at Franklin Elementary school until her retirement to take care of her dear mother. When you look at Bishop Hines one might notice the many.similar features of Miss Galloway; the kind embrace, the lovely, welcoming smile, the caring, engaged look as she talked with you, encouragement for intellect, and the stylish, neatly dressed lady who made time for YOU. They both strived to make certain you knew that you were valued and were a special child of God. We are so fortunate and blessed to have had our lives touched by each of these dynamic and committed ladies.

Grandma's House

O ur grandparent's, Jessie Gwyn and Melissa Gwyn house is a place we will never forget. Some of our fondest memories included time spent with them in their beautiful home. It was like "Grand Central Station" as we gathered every Sunday afternoon for dessert and family fellowship. This was our time of singing around the piano with grandmother singing to the top of her voice.

She was a beautiful lady with bright grey eyes. She was a woman in charge. As an excellent housekeeper, everything was clean and always in place. There was a place for everything except for Grandpapa to smoke. He had to enjoy smoking his pipe outside near the oak tree.

But Bonnie enjoyed our grandparents more than any of us. She started on Saturday evenings, just she and our grandmother in the kitchen. That is where she shared her best cooking secrets. This is where Bonnie developed her love for cooking and where she learned to bake those delicious biscuits, so many came to enjoy.

However, their house was very special in another way, and for another reason. It was on grandmother's back porch that Bonnie practiced her first sermons!

Bonnie was known for her culinary skills which were cultivated in her grandma's kitchen. Mama Dollie (Dorothy Johnson Hines) nurtured her granddaughter's desire to create all kinds of heavenly creations. A pie crust made from scratch was an essential ingredient to Mama Dollie's beloved homemade chocolate pie that Bonnie learned to make under her tutelage and served to the delight of the family; Grandpa, "Papa Jack" (Roscoe Jack Hines), Aunt Rachel Hines Jones (Daddy's only sibling), and Uncle Chilli (Nathaniel Jones).

Church and More Church

Sunday morning worship had two services with preaching, praying, and singing in the church. The second service was held on Grandmother's back steps with Bonnie delivering the sermon and taking up the offering of rocks found in the yard and on the hillside. She was the preacher, and all the sisters cousins and friends were the congregation.

As a teenager, she preached a memorable sermon on a Friday evening on the steps of St. Paul African Methodist Episcopal Church. The topic was "Joy Comes in the Morning." She wore a beautiful white dress. Her parents and family were so very proud of her.

Who knew she would become a preacher!

The Bell Ringer

Sunday was for our family, the most exciting day of the week. The day always started with daddy knocking at the door, calling time to get up girls. It was not hard to open our eyes with the smell of Mamas delicious breakfast in the air. As we took turns buttoning up each other's dress, we talked about how much we had grown overnight. You see, we all wanted to be the Bell Ringer but we could only ring it after we were tall enough to reach the long rope.

Bonnie was the oldest and the tallest. On the short ride to the church, we all wished we could be like Bonnie. All of the children had the same goal . . . to be tall enough to reach the rope and ring the bell. Not once but twice . . . once for Sunday School and then again for Worship service.

What an honor!

After Daddy parked the car, we would all run to the vestibule of the church. There the long rope hung from the ceiling. Nothing was more exciting than to see Bonnie on her tippy toes in her patent leather shoes reaching with all of her strength . . . holding on with all ten fingers. She would rise up in the air . . . back down. And then we would hear the bell ring all over the community.

We all cheered as we too thought about the day we would be tall enough to be . . . The Bell Ringer!

Caring for Others

As time passed, Bonnie came to realize that lots of people were hurting. Some were physically sick; some were spiritually sick, and others were suffering from mental disorders. She decided that something needed to happen, someone should do something to rescue the perishing and care for the dying. That someone became Bonnie. With the right training, she felt that becoming a minister would give her the skills and knowledge she needed to bring comfort and direction to the people through the church.

The saddest day for Bonnie and her family was the loss of Maria, sister number five. It was at this point that Bonnie's real work began . . . to comfort her sisters, as well as their parents and herself!

She would be the comforter.

The Change in Life

Yea, though I walk through the valley of the shadow of death, I will fear no evil: for thou art with me; thy rod and thy staff they comfort me.

—Psalm 23:4

"The Sound of Music"

It's hard to believe that there was a time when Bonnie did not have a church home.

Early in her career, she was blessed with a wonderful position as a family advocate for the United Way Agency. In addition, she was invited to join the Ministry Team at Friendship Missionary Baptist Church in Charlotte, NC. There, she served as a youth minister. She loved both jobs and was able to make the difference she so desired . . . supporting children and families.

However, when both positions ended, she found herself on the outside looking in.

One quiet Sunday morning, while on the steps of the home she and her sisters shared, Bonnie heard church bells ringing. They seemed to beckon her to come.

On the next Sunday, she decided to visit the church and was welcomed with open arms. Soon after, she and her sisters joined the Greenville Memorial AME Zion Church as a family. Praise God! They all became very active, giving of their gifts in Sunday School and the Missionary Department.

From Worship to work

Let the favor of the Lord our God
be upon us, and prosper for us the work
of our hands—O prosper the work
of our hands!

—Psalm 90:17

"From Worship to Work"

Being unemployed can be a blessing. It can provide time for one to explore new possibilities, even look into different career opportunities. This is just what happened to Bonnie in this unique space of her life.

It was at Greenville Memorial AME Zion, her new church, where she met Dr. Mary A. Love, Editor of The Department of Church School Literature for the AME Zion Church. Dr. Love opened a door for Bonnie she did not even know existed.

Among the many responsibilities Dr. Love had as the leader of the department was to build and maintain a team of writers, editors, researchers, and biblical scholars to publish the state-of-the-art literature for our world church. What did she do? She invited Bonnie to join her team. There, Bonnie's position was "ghost writer." This was new and different for Bonnie. It would give her an opportunity to use her well-developed writing skills.

Tenure with Church School Literature opened many doors for Bonnie. During meetings and conferences, she met church leaders from all over the world. She was able to learn and build positive relationships with people throughout our Zion. Little did she know that she would see these people again, and for some, she would become their leader.

The Best Is Yet To Come!

"Belk Teen Board"

Most People do not enjoy going to work!

One last glance into the mirror before I left home. It would be a gross understatement to describe me as being a tiny bit nervous at this moment. Today was the day that I would be presented publicly as a member of the Belk Teen Board for the Belk department store located in Mayberry Mall, Mount Airy, North Carolina.

The average high school girl in Mount Airy was ecstatic to have been selected to serve on the board, but my being a young teen of African-American descent brought even more importance to the day. Driving to the Belk Store, my mind was full of thoughts of how the event would play out. A few butterflies circled in my stomach but were eased by the thought that my best friend, Bonnie, had also been chosen to serve as a Belk Teen.

It seemed that Bonnie and I had been best friends forever! We had attended school as elementary students at J.J. Jones Elementary School. Once the schools in Mount Airy were integrated, Bonnie attended North Surry High School and I attend Mount Airy City High School. She and I were honored that we were the first two (2) black teens selected to serve on the all-female board, but mostly delighted that we both were on the board. We agreed that 'best friends' deserved to be on the board together.

When I arrived at the Belk Store, Bonnie was the first face I noted for it was always a delight to see her beautiful smile as she embraced me with a hello greeting. Of course, we were not placed next to each other but throughout the event, we had the opportunity to chat. As members of the teen board, we were asked to model clothing for store events. What fun we had in choosing the many outfits that we modeled. We took pride in our duties and responsibilities, for we understood that everything that we did as members on the board was a special opportunity to represent our families in the community. However, we knew how to have a few giggles and fun at the same time.

Bonnie and I always had tremendous respect for each other and the thought of competing against each other never surfaced. We worked hard and gained the respect of all; supervisors, co-workers, and customers. I mention customers, for you see with time, Bonnie and I gained additional responsibility. We became very valuable employees and actually worked at the store. Can you guess the first department that we worked in? Hint! Hint! If you ever noticed the stylish shoes that Bonnie always wore; you will guess the correct answer. One of my favorite memories is the time that Bonnie and I worked in the shoe department together, and a huge thunder storm knocked the power out in the store. It was quite dark so much so that Bonnie and I did not see someone sneak and steal shoes off the display tables.

Working with my dear friend, I learned so much about people. I admired her kind gestures expressed to customers. She never criticized and always found a way to make me laugh. There were no bad days working with Bonnie; each day was a bright day with a pleasant smile. So, you see why I enjoyed going to work . . . knowing that I would be working with my best friend, Bonnie. Bonnie enjoyed her time at Belk and became a merchandise buyer for the company. She always excelled at all she did!

—Amy Mittman White

Leadership

I can do all things through him who strengthens me.

—Philippians 4:13 (ESV)

The Pastor

Bonnie served as pastor at a number of churches before she became a Bishop.

Bishop Bonnie was called a meticulous leader who strived for excellence in ministry. With wisdom and grace, she was willing to make necessary changes in leadership and structure in any and all churches to which she was assigned to.

She was brave and unafraid to lead the congregations to a higher standard of service. She was courageous. She was small in stature, but tall in tenacity.

NORTH CAROLINA

Wardell Chapel in Shelby NC was the home church for Ms. Caverness and her brother, Mr. James Hoskins. Here Bishop Bonnie benefitted from working in a small family church that was spiritually strong and financially sound. This was her first appointment as pastor and it was here that she had a firsthand view of the Lay Council and its work in the church and on the district level. St Peters AME Zion Church, was located in the little town of Gastonia NC. The small building was located in the outskirts of the city serving families who had been and some were still employed by the local mills.

This church was known for its exciting spirit-filled services. It was there that Bishop Hines seized the opportunity to strengthen the Deaconess Board. As mothers of the church, she invited them to join her in the office before any and all services. They would form a circle and lay hands on her as they prayed for God's grace and mercy. They constantly prayed for her strength in leading the congregation. During her leadership the deaconess became major players to strengthen the prayer life of the church.

Walls Memorial AME Zion Church, is located in the inner city of Charlotte N. C. It is surround by homeowners and apartment dwellers who enjoy walking or traveling a short distance by car. The church housed a number of "out reach" projects established by previous pastors. Bishop Bonnie's desire was to continue these community efforts and expand them when possible. It was also at this time she began to build her collection of "Light Houses" expressing her desire to shine the light on others and lead them to Christ.

Her effort to take the church leadership team to a higher-level lead her to take the officers on a cruise to the Bahamas. On that ship they enjoyed her bible teaching, daily communion and a motivational speaker.

Even today many attendees speak of this trip as a special time in their spiritual lives.

I worked with Bishop Hines at Walls Memorial as her administrative assistant. I admired her as a leader. She set out to meet her goals and did it with dignity! As pastor, she met the needs of her people and did it with a smile! Bishop Hines was a great teacher and pastor. Lessons learned will take us through life with great memories of her!! | Patricia Williams.

CALIFORNIA
First AME Zion Church

I met Bishop Hines shortly after being promoted to the position of Chief Probation Officer for the Justic Department of LA. It was the most challenging time of my professional career. For me, she became an oasis of peace and understanding. After a day of frustration and disappointment I would find myself in a powerful bible study where she made the bible come alive. There we all learned how the word of God impacts our own lives.

I had been in the church all of my life and had never experienced such Christlike instruction. She was a powerful teacher!

First Church of LA was located in a very fragile community. It functioned like a mission providing for the needs of children and families. It was a large building with a small congregation. But as God would have it, there were some very prominent members who supported the church financially.

They were actors, film writers, and producers (keep in mind, this was LA-the center of the entertainment world.)

However, the pastor was not without her challenges. She had to be strong in leading and sometimes "redirecting" the leadership in the ways of Zion. Her goal was to establish a praying church based upon the Word of God. Sometimes, she was a "force to be reckoned with." As the church grew, she found her greatest gift was her positive people skills along with her Christlike way of problem-solving. Sometimes, they found a way to agree even when they disagreed. Praise God!

Once the announcement was made that our pastor would offer herself to become a Bishop, we were sad and disappointed. We knew that we would lose her and all the good work she had done. But finally, we realized that God wanted her for greater work. At that point I decided I would personally do whatever I could do to support her.

After the election, she was assigned to Africa and I went with her. It was a learning experience I will never forget.

> When I received word of her passing, I was saddened again but encouraged to know that our loss is heaven's gain. To Him be the Glory. | Loretta McCray

The Invitation

Bonnie's first appointment to serve as Pastor was at Waddell Chapel AME Zion Church in Shelby, NC. At this time, she lived in Charlotte, NC with her sisters, two hours away.

One evening after worship service, Mrs. Marilyn Caviness, a devoted member of the church invited her to stay over in her home, instead of driving the distance back to Charlotte in the dark, bad weather. Bonnie eagerly accepted.

That was the beginning of a beautiful, long relationship . . . from church member and pastor to mother and daughter! Mrs. Caviness lived alone. She had everything she needed and was willing to share with Bonnie.

Mrs. Caviness was a beautiful lady inside and out. She was tall in stature and always wore a radiant smile. She loved her church, Waddell Chapel and was especially proud of her new pastor, Rev. Bonnie Hines.

After enjoying a soul-stirring worship service with singing and preaching, she and Bonnie would enjoy a delicious Sunday dinner around her well-appointed dining room table. Mrs. Caviness was an elegant lady and enjoyed the finer things in life.

Interestingly enough, these two dedicated Christian ladies enjoyed shopping! Whenever they traveled to various churches, they always found time to drop in on their favorite boutique or shopping mall.

However, Mrs. Caviness' health continued to decline, and they found their ability to travel became a challenge. But that did not stop Bonnie. She made it a point to take her Godmother everywhere she went.

Connected to the back of her car was a "state-of-the art" wheelchair. . . and away they would go; Church to church, meeting to meeting! To God Be the Glory!

Here "She Served Like a Lamb!!!"

Leadership

As a pastor, she provided quality training for the church leaders. During a church leadership workshop, she often prepared and served refreshments. Her homemade biscuits were always the star of the meal! However, she found great joy in working with the deaconesses. She worked to strengthen their role as "mothers" of the church.

As Bishop, her great desire for all churches was to be "debt-free." She encouraged pastors to develop a plan to pay off the mortgage. The mortgage-burning service was always a highlight for her. No mortgage meant more time to Win Souls for Christ!

"She led like a Lioness."
"She served like a Lamb."
Learning and seeking higher service was her goal!

Teamwork Makes the Dream Work

Rev. Dr. John Ruth

Presiding Elder of The South Atlantic Episcopal District African Methodist Episcopal Zion Church

The Team of SAED Council of Elders working with Bishop Mildred B. Hines to make the Dream Work.

Bishop Mildred B. Hines was elected and consecrated as the 98th Bishop in the line of succession in the AME Zion Church. This was historic! She was the first and only woman elected as Bishop in The Freedom Church. She was assigned as the leader of the South Atlantic Episcopal District. Included in the South Atlantic Episcopal District were four (4) conferences; Georgia, Palmetto, Pee Dee and South Carolina. The nine (9) assigned presiding elders had the awesome responsibility to keep the work of God in high-working order under the leadership of Bishop Hines, as she resided in Los Angeles, California, and experienced severe illness. Team Hines was a God-given and anointed collaboration of presiding elders. They included: Bishop Hines, Bishop Warren M. Brown, and a dedicated Council of Elders!

The task of caring for thousands of members in the South

Atlantic Episcopal District was quite a challenge. However, leadership and teamwork were the orders of the day. One may wonder how it was possible that the South Atlantic Episcopal District nurtured and prospered under the leadership of the first female to be elected to this high office.

There are several reasons attributed to the success of the South Atlantic Episcopal District! Members of the Council of Elders felt that Bishop Hines was a true visionary/dreamer.

She made it clear to the members of the SAED that as the first female to be elected to the highest and most sacred office in The AME Zion Church she had to be successful in all ventures. There was no room for failure! The only way was forward and upward!

Bishop Hines possessed the one quality of a good leader: excellent communication skills. The Council of Elders felt that Bishop Hines had great communication skills. She devised a plan to communicate the needs and wishes of her leadership through frequent weekly meetings with the Council of Elders. She may have been thousands of miles away, but the work of God still had to continue. She may not have been feeling well, but the work of God still had to continue!

The Council of Elders knew that Bishop Hines was a caring person. She cared about the flock that she was leading! This care was communicated to each elder and passed onto the waiting congregations. Therefore, it was easy to carry on, even if she were not physically able to be in person with the SAED!

The members of the SAED Council of Elders were a group of seasoned men and women. They knew and were willing to perform to the highest level because the final assessment would come from God Almighty!

   Yes, it was a known fact that the SAED would prosper even in troublesome times! We knew that God was working with us and through us to make "The Dream Work!"

Service

Bonnie loved serving her congregation, bringing in new members, baptizing babies, and marrying young couples. But her greatest joy was in serving Holy Communion. Her sisters remembered how she would practice with them. Once she threw a ripe watermelon on the ground, busted it into lots of pieces and gave an equal part to each of them. Then she said a prayer and blessed them. They may have been playing, but Bonnie was serious. This was the beginning of her love for serving the Holy Communion.

An Election we will Never Forget

Dr. Barbara Shaw

The General Conference is the most important gathering of the AME Zion Church. Every four years, we gather at a designated site to celebrate and give an account of the work we have done throughout the quadrennium. Delegates from all over the world are present to represent their area.

This is where we elect officers to hold positions to continue the work of the departments and boards that make up the leadership of our world church. At the beginning of the convention, all positions are vacant until new officers are elected or re-elected.

This year was different. It was a time of change. The United States was still at war with Vietnam. Many of our young men were actively serving and some had lost their lives. The economy was unstable and women found they had to step up to the plate and play an even more important role. Not just to provide financially, but to be stronger leaders at home, in the community and in the church.

Women had always made up the majority of household leaders, community volunteers and church workers. However, they were not often church leaders. Never had a woman served a leadership in our highest post—the bishopric. Only men had served in this position, but not this year—the women of the church decided things must change. They believed that of the three positions to be filled, one should be held by a woman. In the past, many women had offered themselves, but none were successful. Not this year!

Ms. Barbara Shaw was serving as the International President of the WH&OM Society of our world church, and under her leadership, the women agreed that by developing and following a strategic plan (including much prayer), we could reach the goal—and we did!

On that day, the women changed a 200-year-old tradition.

On that day Mildred Bernadatta Hines was named Bishop Bonnie Hines. And the rest is history!

To God be the Glory!

Her presence changed the atmosphere. From that day on, when our leaders gathered in their board meeting, she was able to share a different prospective of engaging the children and families in our churches through our world church.

Her absence has left a tremendous void, but not for long. There will be another General Conference and there are still God-fearing women ready to serve as she did.

Praise God . . . The Best Is Yet to Come!

First Female Elected in 226 Years

She had a thirst for learning and a passion for public speaking.

- She was a Noble woman Servant for the Kingdom of God.
- She was a Gentle Counselor and Noble Worker.
- The last two years of Bonnie's Service as a bishop was completely virtual. Because of her fragile health and the international pandemic "COVID-19," she was not able to travel. Through technology, she was able to reach the people from California to the South Atlantic Episcopal District.
- She was successful in leading the Episcopal District into the General Conference with all obligations met.
- Because of her unwavering dedication to the work, she was reassigned to the South Atlantic Episcopal District and served faithfully until God called her home on May 23, 2022.

The Assignment

As the 98th Bishop, she would join the eleven (11) male board members who were charged with the responsibility of leading the twelve (12) Episcopal Districts of our world church.

Her first assignment was to the Western-West Africa Episcopal District.

Her goal, as their episcopal leader, was to visit every church, be it the first church on the district or the last church. She believed they all deserved a visit from their Bishop!

A Very Special Blessing

It was at First AME Zion Church in Los Angeles, California that Bishop Bonnie met Gwendolyn Broomfield, a dedicated member and leader of the church. Gwen was so very proud of her new female pastor and vowed to help and support her in every way she could. She was a special blessing because not only did she understand and work in her local church, but she had a wealth of information and experience about our world church. Gwen had served as a very successful elected officer of the Women's Home and Overseas Missionary Society.

Who knew that Gwen would become the Missionary Supervisor for Bishop Bonnie. Gwen served tirelessly and faithfully until God called her home.

Africa . . . Another World

Africa, Bonnie's first assignment was another world. The weather, travel, the food, the culture—all so very different. Without the support, her work would have almost been impossible.

However, God blessed her graciously with everything she needed. Among the many women who worked tirelessly in the first quadrennium of her tenure, were Dr. Gwendolyn Brumfield and Ms. Charlotte Umoja.

They accompanied her on that first pilgrimage across the sea, her very first assignment. It was their knowledge and experience that allowed her to function as their new leader, new "female" Bishop.

It was Charlotte's understanding and appreciation of the culture of our sisters and others overseas that was a special blessing. The respect she was given from past relationships and time she had already spent in the region opened many doors that could have been very difficult otherwise.

However, it was the years of experience as a Missionary officer that had well prepared Gwen to serve as Bonnie's Missionary Supervisor. Her administrative skills and knowledge enhanced and complemented the challenges she otherwise would have faced.

In addition, more blessings came in the form of sisters and

church members who gave of their time and resources to travel to Africa during the first year. Gwen was there to encourage and support Bonnie all along the way. Loretta McCray blessed her unconditionally as she extended love and understanding in this new world of sisters and brothers. After those first four years, Bonnie returned to the stateside a changed leader. She as one who had served a whole different world—She had served "THE MOTHER LAND!"

Praise God from Whom all Blessings Flow!

The Lighthouse

Most leaders like Bonnie have a hobby, they sometimes collect things that represent what they value. Lighthouses, that is what she loved.

She collected them from all over the world. Some were given to her as gifts and others she purchased for herself. Some houses were made of wood, others of glass and even others were made of paper.

To her, the lighthouse meant a tower of strength, designed to send a bright light to the plane's ships or people. Its purpose is to serve as a beacon or navigational aid . . . to lead the way to safe harbor.

She lived by the words from Jesus, "I am the light of the world . . . Whoever follows me will not walk in darkness . . . But will have the light of life. Your word is a lamp to my feet and a light to my path. You are the light of the world."

—John 8:12.

To Bonnie, the lighthouse was also a symbol of overcoming challenges and adversities. As guidance, it represented a way forward and a help in times of trouble.

Let it Shine . . . Let it Shine . . . Let it Shine! . . .

A Leap of Faith

Surely goodness and mercy shall follow me all the days of my life, and I will dwell in the house of the Lord forever.

—PSALM 23:6

A Very Special Blessing

⚜

It was at First AME Zion Church in Los Angeles, CA that she received the call to offer herself for the position of Bishop; the highest post in our world church. The late Bishop Roy A. Holmes encouraged her to make that big step no female had ever made. With lots of support and encouragement from many church members, officers, and leaders, she began the steps to offer herself through the election process. She often gave credit to the "Women of Zion" for her successful election.

> "Who knew she would win the election and become a Bishop!"

On July 18, 2008, Mildred B. Hines became the first female to be elected to the highest post in the African Methodist Episcopal Zion Church.

After the successful election, there was one big question—What should we call her? Some said, "We should call her 'Rev. Dr. Bishop Hines.'" Others said, "We should call her 'Bishop Mildred Hines.'" Even others thought, "Sister Bishop Hines" or "Mother Bishop Hines." Finally, after munching on one delicious peppermint patty (to calm herself,) she quietly said, "Just call me Bishop Bonnie." Yes, this diminutive woman in the company of these big men, just spoke her piece.

A Life of Service

Bishop Bonnie never married, nor did she have children. However, she was never alone. She was surrounded by her family of sisters and godchildren, that were always actively involved in her ministry.

Who knew the same love and commitment she had for her parents she would give to the church!

"She served like a lamb!"

Footprints Around the World

Africa

Bishop Hines first assignment as bishop was to the Western West Africa Episcopal District, which had over 450 congregations in Ghana, Liberia, Cote d'Ivoire, Togo, and Ivory Coast.

Back to the United States

In 2012, Bishop Hines was assigned to the Southwestern Delta Episcopal District which included congregations in Arkansas, Louisiana, Oklahoma, Mississippi, and West Tennessee. As a result of the sudden death of Bishop Roy A. Holmes in 2013, the New England and the Bahama Islands Conferences of the Northeastern Episcopal District were added to her supervision. She presided over the South Atlantic Episcopal District which includes South Carolina, Pee Dee, Palmetto, Georgia, and South Korea.

A New Home
The House that Bonnie Built

Bonnie was a born builder. She even built her own waterbed! It was leakproof and provided her many peaceful nights of sleep.

However, in 2019, she decided it was time to build a new home—a house where she and her sisters could be together, all under the same roof again. She found a plot of land in the little city of Mount Holly, NC and started drawing up plans. This house would be big enough for each sister to have her own bedroom. Bonnie would have an office connected to her room. It would have lots of bookshelves for all of her books. Outside on the front lawn, beautiful flowers would be planted under a large oak tree, and on the back, there would be a fruit and vegetable garden.

However, God had a different plan. On May 23, 2022, God took Bishop Bonnie to her Heavenly Home. No more pain or sickness . . .

Just Joy, Unspeakable Joy Forevermore!

Reflections in Their Own Words

Bishop Kenneth Monroe Senior Bishop

•

Rev. Dr. Dwight Cannon

•

Bishop Warren M. Brown

•

Mrs. Lovetta Holmes

•

Mrs. Amy M. White

•

Rev. Dr. Valerie A. Maness

•

Mrs. Glenda H. Manning

•

Mrs. JoAnn B. Holmes

•

Dr. Barbara Shaw

•

Ms. Loretta McCray

Living with Great Expectations

Bishop Kenneth Monroe

Senior Bishop of The
African Methodist Episcopal Zion Church

My knowledge of Mildred Bonnie Hines was always distant until the 25th Quadrennial Convention of the Women's Home and Overseas Missionary Society in 2003, held in Rochester, New York. Dr. Bonnie Hines was the Bible Study teacher during the convention. My wife was intrigued by the lessons she taught and spoke with me about her presentation. Unfortunately, I was unable to attend the meetings because I was experiencing an acute gout attack.

Nonetheless, I began to observe her notoriety and followed her ministry. Perhaps that bible study experience launched her desire to excel with great popularity. Not realizing where she might go in the church, it appeared that she was a person who had great possibility. Of course, during the next few years, Dr. Hines moved about the church, preaching and teaching in congregations and annual conferences. In 2008, she was elected the first female bishop in the history of the African Methodist Episcopal Zion Church. Unfortunately, there was some noise regarding her physical health and if she would have the stamina to endure the responsibilities of a bishop. Of course, such a concern can only be legitimate when our faith is unstable. At her death, I was chosen as the eulogist. In choosing the subject for her eulogy, I thought of her faith and the journey she experienced as a leader in the church, "Living with Great Expectations." I raised the importance of employing obedience as a means of demonstrating one's faith.

Bishop Hines was obedient in the faith. She sought to do all she could to live according to the Word of the Lord. Not only did she preach and teach the Word of the Lord, but she sought to embrace and employ what she taught. She was a student of the Bible. Her relationship with the Lord was precious to her, and it would have caused her much grief to violate that relationship. Without question, there were moments of discomfort and difficulty, but she kept the faith. There were times of disappointment and discouragement, but she kept the faith. Many times when our expectations have not materialized as quickly as we think they should have, we will violate our faith. Bishop Hines did not allow her times of disappointment or even her moments of discouragement to violate her faith in God. It always appeared that her confidence in God was constant. Without question, her faith was constantly being hammered by the blows of the world as well as the deterioration of her physical body. Yet, in the midst of her battles, she learned to be still and listen for direction and comfort from the Lord.

No doubt, Bishop Hines understood the concept of obedience to the faith. She understood that she did not have to lose heart in the midst of trial, instead she knew to be faithful. She did not have to waddle in pity when she was having a difficult time. She understood the importance of just keeping the faith. She knew not to turn to the world to get an answer to the problems she was facing, realizing it would be best to just keep the faith.

Bishop Hines lived 24,487.75 days! Perhaps during her days on this earth, she had opportunities to learn more earnestly to appreciate each new day. Please understand that it is not appropriate to enter a new day bringing the old baggage from the old day or the day before. Bonnie Hines realized that she was about to move from time to eternity. In the process of her transition, she had to take off anxiety; take off trial and tribulation; take off the troubles of this world, take off sickness and disease and put on a new spirit, and get into a new position with God. Even though she understood the importance of praise and worship, her approach to worship would change. I am not sure if she realized it or not, but Bishop Hines was preparing to embrace a different, redeeming and transforming new day. Her future is now filled with blessings. She is able to recognize and acknowledge this new day God has given her. She did not get to this day because of her goodness or because of her intelligence. She was able to arrive at this new day because of her faithfulness to God and the church. But thank God for a new day! Bishop Mildred Bonnie Hines, enjoy the new day God has given you. Your expectations have now been realized!

A Tribute to Bishop Mildred "Bonnie" Hines

Rev. Dr. Dwight Cannon

Executive Director of the Department of Global Missions and Editor in Chief for The Missionary Seer of The African Methodist Episcopal Zion Church

O nly one woman can rightfully claim to be the mother of the entire African Methodist Episcopal Zion Church—Bishop Mildred "Bonnie" Hines!

We suspend this moment in our day to mourn the earthly transition of our mother to her ethereal and celestial place of repose (rest and peace) in the sky. Rest in Peace, Bishop Mildred "Bonnie" Hines!

We pause as we pine the pioneer of female preachers, who dared to break the proverbial glass ceiling and was left to clean up the shattered glass broken by her success—Bishop Mildred "Bonnie" Hines!

She was the first female Bishop in Zion Methodism; the first female to preside over the mission fields of Western West Africa (Ghana, Liberia, Togo & Cote D'Ivoire); the first female to become President of the Board of Bishops; the first female bishop to preside over the Southwestern Delta Episcopal District; the first female bishop presiding over the South Atlantic Episcopal District—Bishop Mildred "Bonnie" Hines!

We laud this lovely lady who was unapologetically female and had the audacity to announce to the Father's of the Church—"LADY ON BOARD—LADY ON THE BOARD OF BISHOPS!"

I was blessed to share confidence with Bishop Hines as we encouraged each other—both needing a kidney, both type O and both believing God for our healing—well Bishop Mildred "Bonnie" Hines got her healing—I await my own healing!

So, sleep on (Ghana, Twi . . . Ko Ko Da). Mother—your house is in order!

So, Sleep on (Ivory Coast, French . . . va te coucher-Maman) Mother, the worldly cares are no bother!

So, Sleep on Mother, Zion will remember you as feeding her branches and leaves as a nurturing vine!

So, sleep on Mother—our very own Bishop Mildred "Bonnie" Hines!

In Togo, I can hear them saying to our mother, Goodbye (Do agbe.) WE WILL MEET AGAIN (Mia dogo!)

Reflections on Bishop
Mildred "Bonnie" Hines

Bishop Warren M. Brown

To begin with I am grateful for the invitation to give thought to my reflections on the personal and working relationship sharded with Bishop Mildred Hines the 98th Bishop elected in the line of succession of the African Methodist Episcopal Zion Church. History cannot overlook the fact that she was the first and only woman elected to this high and holy position. (As of the writing of this article).

On a personal reflection I came to know Bishop Hines years before either of us was elected a Bishop, myself August 1996, and she July, 2008. The personal relationship took root and became the foundation for our professional relationship. Immediately following her election and assignment to Western West Africa Episcopal District. Aurelia, my wife, and I invited Bishop Hines and Dr. Gwendolyn Broomfield, the Missionary Supervisor to spend several days with us in Washington, DC to assist them in preparing for their new leadership role. In my reflection the time was well spent and enjoyable. One thing was clear, Bishop Hines was her own person and made her own decisions regarding her work. She did on occasion ask my opinion, while doing whatever she thought best.

Upon my retirement July 2012, Aurelia and I moved to Atlanta Ga which is in the South Atlantic Episcopal District, which was assigned to Bishop Hines in 2016, and she became my Bishop.

This move threw us into a new relationship, which was not problematic, but different. Soon afterwards illness invaded her body, and it was my duty to support and assist her as she desired. I recall the day she called asking me to assist her. I am happy to write that we found the level of trust that made it easy to be become part of her team and to serve her and the Episcopal Area so as not to restrict the stability of the Episcopal area. Two things became clear, one her illness did not affect her thoughtfulness attention to details.

While travel was restricted, she was still in charge. Health challenges did not weaken her leadership style. At the same time, she was open to suggestions; it was easy to cover for her. It was important to me not to get ahead of her, ours was a team effort on all fronts. I must say that the Presiding Elders and Pastors of South Atlantic District and District Officers did their part to ensure there were no leaks or breaks.

When God opened the door for Bishop Hines to return to Him, there was still a sense of grace.

Illness was not conquered and she was not defeated. "Where, O death, is your victory? Where, O grave is your sting? The sting of death is sin . . . But thanks be to God! He gives us the victory through our Lord Jesus Christ" l Corinthians 15: 55-56.

l close this brief statement with recognition of the family of Bishop Hines, who sought to protect her when she could not make her own decisions. l salute them for covering her at the time of greatest need. Let the record reflect that it was my honor to assist my sister in Christ, because it was right and l wanted to do it.

—Bishop Warren M. Brown

Tribute to the Right Reverend Mildred "Bonnie" Hines
(1955-2022)

Mrs. Lovetta J. Holmes
Missionary Supervisor

At the 48th Session of the General Conference of the African Methodist Episcopal Zion Church, which convened in Atlanta, Georgia in 2008, amid a growing demand that women have a greater say in its decision-making, a historical and significant revolution took place during the election process. This broke up the all-male hierarchy of the Board of Bishops when delegates elected the denomination's first and only female bishop, to date.

Yet, long before she achieved this personal milestone, Rev. Mildred "Bonnie" Hines was a pioneer of change with a gentle, but powerful voice. Evident was the drive of her religious convictions concerning the equality, integrity, and capacity of women to be leaders in the Church. As a bishop, she was an effective agent for developing excellence in leadership among clergy and lay people. She desired nothing short of a winning team for her ministry, a fact which was at the forefront of her Episcopal agenda.

In spite of her tireless search for solutions to the crisis of leadership that the Church perennially undergoes, her personal ambition was tempered by her absolute faith and trust in God's will and way for herself, for those who were under her direct charge, and for the Church at-large. She was often heard to say, "May He send forth His Light and His Truth and may they guide us as we seek to do His Will and do it His Way."

A woman warrior "on the battlefield" for the Lord has left us, and we are bereft of her representation and advocacy. We, in the AME Zion Church, have felt this loss personally, collectively, and ecumenically. Like our fallen pioneer, the Right Reverend Mildred "Bonnie" Hines, may we recognize the strength and capacity of women for leadership in the Church. May we have the courage of our convictions, be as brave and tireless, and march as steadfastly in the will and way of our God.

A Tribute to my Childhood Friend . . . Bishop
Mildred "Bonnie" Hines

Mrs. Amy M. White

The greatest jewel in life is having a best friend. My jewel was "Bonnie" Hines, officially known as, Bishop Mildred "Bonnie" Hines. Bonnie and I were childhood friends and maintained a beautiful relationship. As young girls, we attended school together until the integration of schools resulted in our attending separate schools. Integration did not keep Bonnie and me separated, as we saw each other at church programs. Bonnie and I attended different churches, but I loved to attend the various church programs and hear the joyous songs as the Hines family serenaded the people.

As teenagers, Bonnie and I worked together at the local Belk Department Store where we were the first two black students to work at the store. Thereafter, we each left Mount Airy to begin our lifelong careers. I have to admit that we did not have emails or cell phones, so our communications with each other ceased to a minimum. One day, I had an acquaintance mention this phenomenal female minister in the AME Zion Church connection. You can only imagine my happiness to hear that the minister was my dear friend, Bonnie.

What a glorious day when Bonnie and I reunited. We talked and laughed like we were young girls again. I loved her dearly and was humbled to be her friend. We would telephone each other and chat for over an hour. Each telephone call was so enduring and colorful as she shared details of her adventures and travels. I recognized that she was a very busy and sought-out person and was honored that she made time for me. I was very proud of her as an individual and her many accomplishments. I made every attempt to attend church services for which she was involved in North Carolina. When I entered the sanctuary and she noticed my entry, and blew me a kiss and often signaled for me to come to the side of the pulpit so that we could share a quick embrace. I was even more humbled by her actions, whereby, she openly announced to the congregation that her best friend was present.

    Shortly after our reunion, I coordinated a Women's Day program at my church. I invited Bonnie to be the guest speaker for the program, if her schedule would permit. Of course, she accepted the invitation and delivered a beautiful, inspiring message. As I introduced Bonnie as the speaker, I shared a synopsis of our journey as friends. In particular, I spoke of how, as a friend, she always made me laugh—she never spoke unkindly of others.

    Several years ago, Bonnie's mother was in the hospital during the Thanksgiving holiday. I told my friend that I would not allow her and her family to eat hospital food on Thanksgiving Day. Yielding to my insistence, Bonnie, her father and two sisters, Charlotte and Renita joined my family for dinner. Thereafter, each year, they accepted the open invitation to be a part of our Thanksgiving celebration and became a new addition to my village. This year, 2023, Charlotte and Renita kindly invited me to their lovely home. I miss my dear friend immensely, but will be forever thankful for having her in my life. I am mindful of the closing song at her beautiful 'Home-going Ceremony'... "It is well. It is well with my soul."

A Tribute to My Friend and My Leader

Rev. Dr. Valerie A. Maness

Only a woman who is truly called by God will even consider stepping into the sacred path of ministry. It's a step you take, knowing the adversities that confront you, but never realizing how grave they really are. Once you accept this calling, it's good to have a mentor who can support you through the journey. To me, The Rt. Rev. Mildred Bernadatta Hines was just that. As time passed, she became even more—a sister, a confidant, one to look up to.

I first met the then Rev. Hines at a conference where she was a workshop leader for women in ministry. I cannot say how impressed I was with her presentation. When I asked my father in the ministry who she was, he informed me that she was the one who would become the first female bishop in the AME Zion Church. He advised me to get to know her and learn from her what he could not teach me. I did just that.

Only God knew where this friendship would lead. I watched her intently as she moved around the church, noting how she stood strong and did not seem to be intimidated by anyone. I admired how she maintained her femininity and did not try to be anything she was not. I followed her as she conducted seminars, workshops, preached, and moved around Zion. Then the moment came when she announced that God had called her to seek the office of a bishop. My heart was overwhelmed.

I was there to celebrate both her campaign and God's victory as she was elevated to the highest office in our denomination. Even then, she did not change. She remained the same as she had been, never making me feel that I could not approach her. She acknowledged my presence whenever she saw me.

When she was assigned to Africa, I wanted so badly to go with her, but that was not God's will. Little did I know that He was preparing me for a later time.

After the passing of my Presiding Bishop, the Board of Bishops assigned her to preside over our area until the next General Conference. My soul flipped. Finally, we would work together! At that time, I was the Conference Secretary, so I knew we'd be in close contact.

It was a joy unspeakable, those sacred moments of sharing. She would regularly have "Girl Talks" at the episcopal residence with the female clergy. It was a time of sharing, but more importantly, a time of gleaning from one who had taken many of the hard knocks we would be spared. She would spread her skirt and allow us to sit around her as she shared the wisdom, knowledge and understanding God had given her.

I gleaned so much from her, so it was no wonder that I did not hesitate to relocate to South Carolina when she was appointed. Going to help my friend, my sister, my mentor, was no problem at all. Little did I know that God was placing me to be where Bishop Hines would need me most!

Her Mentors and Mothers

Mrs. JoAnn B. Holmes
and Mrs. Glenda H. Manning

We were Bonnie's self-appointed godmothers and had the pleasure of welcoming Bonnie and her sisters to the Greenville Memorial AME Zion Church family. Being a licensed experienced preacher, she was indeed a wonderful and much-needed addition to our growing congregation.

Her willingness to meet new people was exciting as she visited other church members in the district. She loved to drive and chaperone her senior mothers to meetings and functions on the District and Annual Conference Levels.

From the time she was appointed to the first church in Shelby, NC, we always made a point to worship with Bonnie and her congregations throughout North Carolina and California. She was always a gracious hostess, sharing a meal she prepared herself.

One of our fondest memories was of her pop-up visits. After the election, even in her busy schedule, she would take the time to visit. Sometimes, she would just appear at the door, squeezing in a moment between meetings. She was always welcome and she knew it. When we were blessed with more time, we would stop by our favorite restaurant for breakfast that turned into lunch. Time would pass by quickly as we caught up on family, church, and more.

We were not privileged to travel with her to Africa, but are truly grateful to those sisters and friends who were.

Attending her Homegoing Service was, for us, a once-in-a lifetime privilege in that we saw her life come full circle—"Our Child"—"Zion's Finest"—Having done the best work in her short life . . . And now on her way to Glory!

To God Be Praised!

Honoring
BISHOP MILDRED B. HINES

I am deeply moved and find it difficult to adequately express my gratitude and admiration for the late Bishop Hines. I recall being present in Atlanta, Georgia, on July 18, 2008 at the 48th General Conference of The African Methodist Episcopal Zion Church as she was elected the 98th bishop in the line of succession of The A.M.E. Zion Church.

I could not have imagined that I would one day pastor in the Western Episcopal District, where, by divine arrangement, Bishop Hines would be the bishop in residence.

Our bond was profound; a mutual affection and respect blossomed between us. I had the privilege to serve her in various capacities, both in person and where she needed to remotely served the wonderful people of the South Atlantic Episcopal District. Her calls, whether to record a sermon or to join in worship with the First Church Pasadena family, were always cherished moments.

I am profoundly honored that her final sermon was delivered at First Church in Pasadena, California. Her message, titled "Bend but Don't Snap," Matthew 28:16-20; remains a source of inspiration. The privilege to offer final prayers by her bedside as she transitioned into the glorious presence of God, granted to me by her family, is something I hold close to my heart.

Zion has indeed lost a giant in the passing of Bishop Hines. Her legacy of strength, wisdom, and grace looms large, a beacon of light and inspiration for us all. As we approach the next General Conference, it is my earnest prayer that the church remembers the remarkable trail she blazed. May we see the fulfillment of her legacy in the election of another female bishop, continuing the journey of diversity and equity in the life of our cherished church.

Let us continue to pray, trusting that God will guide the AME Zion church forward, always keeping us anchored in faith and unity."

REV. JERRED MCDANIEL, SENIOR PASTOR
FIRST A.M.E. ZION CHURCH PASADENA CALIFORNIA

Who Was Bishop Mildred "Bonnie" Hines?

The Etymology of the Right Reverend Bishop Mildred "Bonnie" Hines

Mildred—The name of a famous eighth-century saint, derives its roots from the English and Old English meaning "Gentle and Strength," which together is a very compassionate personality . . .

Bonnie—with English and common Scottish roots, simply means "pretty" and "beautiful" . . .

Hines—name with German, Irish, and English roots, means "God is Gracious" and "Home of the King!"

Together, she is and has always been, our "Queen Mother" . . . who is both "beautiful" and "pretty" as she led, worshipped, worked and presided with "Gentle Strength" and "Amazing Grace!" As she was in life, she is in eternal life, always at home with the KING!

Done this the 9th day of July in the year of our Lord, 2023.

Respectfully Submitted,
Rev. Dr. Sheldon R. Shipman, Pastor
Greenville Memorial AME Zion Church

What You May or May Not Know About Bonnie

She loved York peppermint patties.

She loved funny jokes.

She loved books of all kinds.

She loved sports.

Her favorite football team was the Dallas Cowboys.

She loved fine Writing instruments "Mont Blanc."

She believed in second chances.

She did not like carrots.

She played a trumpet and the snare drums.

Her favorite song was, "I am Thine O Lord."

She was a fashion buyer for Belk Department Stores.

Her favorite color was green.

Her shoe size was 7 1/2 narrow.

She was 5 feet 4 inches tall.

Her favorite shade of nail polish was red.

She loved cooking and watching the cooking channel.

Her favorite season of the year was summer.

She loved building things.

She loved Gardening

She loved the church.

She loved children.

She loved her nieces and nephews.

She loved her family; they were very important to her.

She loved the Lord.

Bishop Bonnie and Former President Barak Obama were elected the same year. (2008)

Official Documents

Education, Work, Church, and Civic Service

Bishop Hines received her education in the public county schools in Surry County, North Carolina. She credited Miss Virginia Galloway, her first-grade teacher, for instilling in her a thirst for learning and a passion for speaking. Her favorite subjects were English, chemistry, history and home economics at North Surry High School. After receiving an academic and athletic scholarship, Bishop Hines attended Mars Hill College in Mars Hill, North Carolina, where she received a Bachelor of Arts Degree in Fashion Merchandising and Home Economics Education. She received her Master of Arts in Psychology from the University of North Carolina at Greensboro. She then was awarded a Master of Divinity from The Interdenominational Theological Center in Atlanta, GA and Certification in Clinical Pastoral Counseling from the Colgate Rochester School of Divinity in Rochester, NY. Ultimately, she received the Doctor of Ministry from the Interdenominational Theological Center in Atlanta, GA.

Her lay profession was as a Senior Buyer for Belk Department Stores. She served as an Office Assistant and Ghostwriter for our Department of Church School Literature for the AME Zion Church. Developing for greater life and works of ministry, she served in Youth Ministry at Friendship Missionary Baptist Church in Charlotte, NC. Later, as a member of Greenville Memorial AME Zion Church, she grew exponentially working in WH&OMS, Christian Education, Lay Council, Mass Choir, and became an Associate in Ministry in this season. The journey heightened as she was sent as Supply Pastor to Waddell Chapel AME Zion Church, Shelby, NC, later becoming pastor. She then pastored St. Peter's Tabernacle AME Zion Church of Gastonia, NC; Walls Memorial AME Zion Church of Charlotte, NC, and First AME Zion Church of Los Angeles, CA. Bishop Hines was elected in Atlanta, GA on July 18, 2008 at the 48th Quadrennial General Conference of the AME Zion Church. She is the first and only female to be elected to the Episcopacy in the 226-year history of the denomination, and on February 20, 2013, she became the first female to head the AME Zion Church when she was elected President of the Board of Bishops.

Bishop Hines was a member of Alpha Kappa Alpha Sorority, Inc. (AKA). She was a Life Member of the NAACP, a Legacy Life Member of the National Council of Negro Women, as well as a member of the Los Angeles unit of Church Women United. Prior to the elevation to the Episcopacy, Bishop Hines served as a member of the President's Advisory Board for the University of Southern California. She was also a faculty member for University of Southern California's School of Religion Center for Religion and Civic Culture, where she taught Leadership Development classes to empower clergy and lay leaders, assisting them to expand their vision for community development and social engagement projects. She sat on several boards, including the Southern Christian Leadership Conference, Los Angeles Council of Churches and the Traditional Black Methodist Churches, of Los Angeles.

Resolution of Comfort
on the Service of Triumph for

The Right Reverend Mildred "Bonnie" Hines,

Greenville Memorial AME Zion Church

B Behold, I show you a mystery that we shall not all sleep, but we shall all be changed. In a moment, in the twinkling of an eye, at the last trump; for the trumpet shall sound, and the dead shall be raised incorruptible, and we shall be changed. I Corinthians 15: 51–52.

Whereas, the Right Reverend Mildred B. Hines, affectionately known to many as Bishop "Bonnie" Hines, humbly surrendered here on earth upon completion of the tasks assigned to her hands to join the immortal ranks of those who have gone before.

Whereas, the Right Reverend Mildred B. Hines, was a devoted family woman, the first of five daughters—Renita, Marcia, Charlotte, and Maria (deceased)—born to Roscoe and JoAnn Gwyn Hines of Mt. Airy, North Carolina, a family town, in the beautiful rural surroundings of Surry County.

Whereas, the Right Reverend Mildred B. Hines, was a devout

member of the Greenville Memorial A. M. E. Zion Church, where she confessed Christ and served faithfully as an Associate Minister, a leader in the Christian Education Department, a member of the Missionary Society, Lay Council, and Mass Choir until she responded to God's call to begin the journey of her pastoral ministry at Waddell Chapel A.M.E. Zion Church (Shelby, NC), St. Peter's Tabernacle A.M.E. Zion Church (Gastonia, NC), Walls Memorial A.M.E. Zion Church (Charlotte, NC) and finally, First A.M.E. Zion Church in Los Angeles, C.A., prior to her election to the episcopacy.

Whereas, the Right Reverend Mildred B. Hines, was elected the 98th bishop in the line of succession of the A.M.E. Zion Church on July 18, 2008 at the 48th General Conference held in Atlanta, Georgia, becoming the FIRST and ONLY FEMALE to be elected to the episcopacy in the 222nd year history of our denomination, and on February 20, 2013, became the FIRST FEMALE to head the A.M.E. Zion Church when she was elected President of the Board of Bishops, we graciously salute the legacy of this pioneering prelate and distinguished woman of God.

Whereas, the Right Reverend Mildred B. Hines, was a member of Alpha Kappa Alpha Sorority, Inc. (AKA), a Life Member of the NAACP, a Legacy Life Member of the National Council of Negro Women (NCNW), and served on the board of the Southern Christian Leadership Conference (SCLC) and served as a member of the President's Advisory Board for the University of Southern California.

Whereas, the Right Reverend Mildred B. Hines, was a woman of many talents and strengths, and her life speaks volumes to those who knew and loved her and the auspicious work she did to bring the lost to Christ and to build His kingdom.

Therefore, be it resolved that our dear beloved Reverend Mother, the Right Reverend Mildred B. Hines, will be sorely missed among her family, the Board of Bishops, the entire denomination, her home church, her friends, colleagues, World Methodism, and others.

Be it resolved that the Right Reverend Mildred B. Hines has gone on to join the ranks of the immortal. Indeed, she has fought the good fight of faith . . . receive your crown of life.

Be it also resolved that a copy of this resolution be given to the Hines family to treasure with her other memoirs and a copy becomes a permanent record of the Greenville Memorial African Methodist Episcopal Zion Church records and archives.

Done this the 31st day of May, in the year of our Lord 2022.

Respectfully submitted,

Rev. Dr. Sheldon R. Shipman, Pastor, Mr. Terrain D. Gill, Trustee Board, Chairman, Sister Katie Weldon, Steward Board, Chairwoman.

Obituary

The Right Reverend Mildred "Bonnie" Hines (May 6, 1955 – May 23, 2022) is the first of five daughters—Renita, Marcia, Charlotte, and Maria (deceased) born to Roscoe and JoAnn Gwyn Hines of Mount Airy, North Carolina, a rural, family town. The home of her grandparents, Jess and Melissa Gwyn was one of the three gathering sites for members of the community; the other two were the church and the school.

Bishop Hines received her schooling in the public county schools in Surry County, North Carolina. She credits Miss Virginia Galloway, her first-grade teacher, for instilling in her a thirst for learning and a passion for speaking.

Her favorite subjects were English, Chemistry, History and Home Economics at North Surry High School. After receiving an academic and athletic scholarship, Bishop Hines attended Mars Hill College in Mars Hill, NC, where she received a Bachelor of Arts Degree in Fashion Merchandising and Home Economics Education. She received her Master of Arts in Psychology from the University of North Carolina at Greensboro. She then was awarded a Master of Divinity from the Interdenominational Theological Center in Atlanta, GA and certification in Clinical Pastoral Counseling from the Colgate Rochester School of Divinity in Rochester, NY. She also was awarded the Doctor of Ministry from the Interdenominational Theological Center in Atlanta, GA.

She served as an office assistant and ghostwriter for the Department of Church School Literature for the A. M. E. Zion Church. Her lay profession was as a Senior Buyer for Belk Department Stores. Bishop Hines was elected in Atlanta, GA on July 18, 2008 at the 48th Quadrennial General Conference of the A. M. E. Zion Church. She is the first and only female to be elected to the Episcopacy in the 226-year history of the denomination, and on February 20, 2013 she became the first female to head the A. M. E. Zion Church when she was elected President of the Board of Bishops. Bishop Hines is a member of Alpha Kappa Alpha Sorority, Inc. (AKA). She is a Life Member of the NAACP, a Legacy Life Member of the National Council of Negro Women as well as a member of the Los Angeles unit of Church Women United. Prior to her elevation to the Episcopacy, Bishop Hines served as a member of the President's Advisory Board for the University of Southern California. She also was a faculty member for USC's School of Religion Center for Religion and Civic Culture, where she taught Leadership Development classes to empower clergy and lay leaders, assisting them to expand their vision for community development and social engagement projects. She sat on several boards, including the Southern Christian Leadership Conference, the Los Angeles Council of Churches, and the Traditional Black Methodist Churches of Los Angeles. Bishop Hines' first assignment as Bishop was to the Western West Africa Episcopal District, which included over 450 congregations in

Ghana, Liberia, Cote' d'Ivoire and Togo. Bishop Hines in 2012 was assigned supervision of the Southwestern Delta Episcopal District which included congregations in Arkansas, Louisiana, Oklahoma, Mississippi, Texas and West Tennessee. After the sudden death of Bishop Roy A. Holmes in May 2013, the New England and the Bahamas Islands Conferences of the North Eastern Episcopal District were added to her supervision. She has presided over the South Atlantic Episcopal District which includes South Carolina, Pee Dee, Palmetto, Georgia and since 2016, and assigned Korea in 2020.

She is survived by her sisters: Renita Hines, Mount Holly, NC; Marcia Hines Parrish (Percy) Dallas, TX; Charlotte Hines Wallace; Mount Holly, NC; nieces and nephews, Monica Gordon, Las Vegas, Charles Wallace, Asheville, NC; Jayda Parrish, NY, Jazmine Parrish, Dallas, TX; Spencer Pope, Charlotte, NC; Patrick Pope, Jr. (Brittany), Dallas, TX a host of relatives and friends. She was preceded in death by her parents, sister Maria Hines Pope, and infant brother Roscoe Johnson Hines, Jr.

His purposes will ripen fast, Unfolding every hour.

The bud will have a bitter taste, but sweet will be the flower.

The Prelude
Order of Service
Bishop Darryl B. Starnes, Presiding

The Processional	Abide with Me!
The Call to worship	Bishop George D. Crenshaw
The Invocation	Bishop Seth O. Lartey
The Hymn of Praise	"When I Can Read My Title Clear"
The Affirmation of Faith	The Apostles' Creed
	Bishop Michael A. Frencher, Sr.
The Old Testament	Job 19:23-27
	Bishop Warren M. Brown
The Gloria Patri	
The New Testament	2 Corinthians 5:1-10
	Bishop W. Darin Moore
The Prayer of Comfort	Bishop Brian R. Thompson
The Music of Inspiration	The Men of Zion

Tributes

Southwest Delta Episcopal District Rev. Dr. Floyd Chambers

New England Annual Conference Rev. Dr. Terry L. Jones, Sr.

South Atlantic Episcopal District Rev. Lelar B. Johnson

W H & O M Society Mrs. Sandra Crowder, International President

Department of Global Missions Dr. Dwight B. Cannon, Secretary

Board of Bishops	Bishop Dennis V. Proctor
Music of Inspiration	The Boyd Trio
The Presentation of the Eulogist	
The Hymn of Preparation	"I am Thine, O Lord"
The Eulogy	Bishop Kenneth Monroe, Presiding Bishop Eastern N. C. Episcopal District Senior Bishop – A. M. E. Zion Church
The Music of Inspiration "It Is well With My soul"	Rev. Vanessa McLamb
The Recessional	
The Interment	
The Benediction	Bishop Kenneth Monroe

With Thanks

Acknowledgements

Before another word is read and another thought is reflected . . . we want to say THANK YOU to all who gave of their time and resources to make this book possible and to bless the memory of our "Bonnie."

If by chance you gave in your own way and find that you name is not listed here, know that our oversight was not intentional. Our heartfelt thanks go out to everyone who gave of themselves and their talents so graciously.

To all of God's children we say Thank You!

To The Board of Bishops.

Retired Bishop George E. Battle, Jr.
Retired Bishop Warren M. Brown
Retired Bishop George W. Walker, Sr.

Mrs. Glenda Manning
Mrs. JoAnn Holmes
Ms. Loretta Mc Cray
Dr. Barbara Shaw
Mrs. Amy White
Ms. Lisa Barkley

Rev. Dr Dwight B. Cannon
Dr. Mary Love
Rev. Dr. Sheldon R. Shipman
Mrs. Patricia Williams
Mrs. Monica Pitts
Ms. Beverly Hunt

Team Hines

You blessed our sister, Bishop Hines in so many ways. We are grateful for the support and love you gave our family and to her as your Bishop during the time she spent with you in the South Atlantic Episcopal District.

MISSIONARY SUPERVISORS:
Dr. Gwendolyn Brumfield (deceased), Mrs. Lovetta J. Holmes

RESIDENT BISHOPS:
Bishop Warren M. Brown, Bishop Louis Hunter, Sr. (deceased)

ADMINISTRATIVE ASSISTANT:
Ms. Jeanetta Crittenden LA

PRESIDING ELDERS:
Rev. Dr. John Paul Ruth, Rev. Reginald M. Morton, Rev. Lelar Johnson, Rev. Dr. Victor C. Wilson, Rev. Dr. Alvin W. McLamb, Rev. Dr. Otha L. Smith, Rev. Sharon Browning, Rev. Dr. Robert E. Christian, Sr., Rev. Dr. Sandra K. Benton, Rev. Eldrin Morrison

RECEPTIONIST:
Rev. Sandra Sistare

ACCOUNTING:
Mrs. Rosetta J. Dunham, Mrs. Annette Currey

MEDIA:
Mr. Tremaine Miller

PRAYER COORDINATORS:
Rev. Thelma Gordan, Rev. Dr. Roe Nall

CLEANING:
Ms. Phyllis McCullough, Ms. Rosie Hyman

COOKS:
Mrs. Johnnie Mae Coleman, Mrs. Lolita Dixon

RESIDENCE CARE TAKERS:
Rev. Lloyd Snipes, Rev. William Norris Long, Rev. Raymond Massey, Mr. James C. Barber.

* All Pastors, Clergy, and Laity of the South Atlantic Episcopal District

Special Thanks to

Miss Kenashia Thompson "Bishop's Shadow"
Rev. Dr. Geroge McKain II, Director of Public Affairs and Social Concerns of the AME Zion Church and staff

The Star of Zion

Department of Global Missions and Missionary Seer, AME Zion Church Department of Church School Literature African Methodist Episcopal Zion Church

Glossary of Terms

Glossary of Terms

Adversity	A condition of trouble or difficulty.
Africa	The Motherland.
A.M.E Zion	The official name of our denomination—African Methodist Episcopal Zion Church.
Assignment	The appointment made by the Episcopal Co Committee.
Biography	A written story of the facts and events of a person's life.
Bishop	The highest level of leadership; elected by the people; blessed by God for years of service.
Character	Strong moral qualities.
Christian	Believers of Jesus Christ.
Civic	Up or having to do with citizens or citizenshi.
Communion	The worship service commemorating the Last Supper.
Congregation	The gathering of members for worship and work.
Contribution	Something that is given or donated.
Deaconnesses	Women set aside—Mothers of the church, responsible for preparing and serving the communion table.
Debt Free	To have no church mortgage—owned by the congregation.
Dedication	Service set aside for a purpose with blessings
District	A group of churches led by a Presiding Elder.

Documents	A written or printed paper that gives factual information or proof of something.
Episcopal	Describes a denomination led by a Bishop.
Episcopal District	The area churches led by a Bishop.
Election	The democratic process for choosing a leader.
Epilogue	Closing remarks in a book.
Etymology	The history of a word shown by tracing it or its parts back to the earliest known forms and meanings, both in its own language and any other language from which it or its parts may have been taken.
Excellence	The condition of being very good or outstanding.
Foreword	The first words to support and announce the book.
Faith	Belief in divine order.
General Conference	The gathering of all our world church leaders held every 4 years.
Glass Ceiling	The unseen limit for a leader.
God	Our Heavenly Father.
God-Fearing	Someone who is religious and tries to live in the way they believe God wishes them to.
Grace	The kindness or help of God.
Grand Central Station	Commuter rail terminal located at 42nd Street and Park Avenue in Midtown Manhattan, New York City.
Homegoing	A funeral tradition in the United States. African-American community that celebrates the loved one's release from this life in a reunion with God.

Holy Communion	The most important religious service in the Christian church in which people share Bread and Wine as a symbol of the Last Supper before the death of Christ.
Honesty	Tell the truth.
Humility	Reducing oneself to raise up others; thinking less of me and more of thee.
Invitation	To extend the welcome.
Jesus	Our Lord and Savior.
Kingdom	Country, state, or territory ruled by a king or queen.
Love	Strong feelings of affection for another person or thing.
Methodist	A member of a Protestant Christian religious denomination developed from the teachings. of John Wesley in the early eighteenth century.
Meticulous	Very careful or precise.
Minister	A person authorized to perform or help at the religious services of some religions.
Mortgage	A written agreement by which a bank or other institution agrees to lend money so that one can buy property.
Navigate	Move through challenging times.
Official	Approved by the public.
Ordained	To admit to the clergy as a priest, minister, or rabbi in a formal ceremony.
Perish(ing)	To die or be destroyed by violence or in some other way that is not natural.
Preach	To share the message of the Bible.
Preside	Provide leadership over a group of believers.

Pulpit	The raised platform in a house of worship where a member of the clergy stands to speak to the gathered people.
The Question	Will you feed my sheep?
Reflection	To look back; share thoughts of the past.
Resolution	It's a formal declaration of the relationship between the deceased and their church or community organization. It honors the good works and/or spiritual commitments of the deceased.
Segregation	The practice of separating people according to groups, especially racial groups.
Sermon	A talk given during a religious service.
Service	The art of caring for others.
Shepherd	A person who guides and protects.
Supervision	Leadership that provides guidance.
Testimony	Spiritual witness given by the Holy Ghost, or the sharing of one's salvation and God's grace with others.
Trailblazer	One who leads the way, traveling a path not covered.
The Call	A Word of direction from God or an invitation to preach the Word of God.
Understand	To hear, learn, be told, or gather. To get the meaning, nature, or importance of a subject.
Victory	Move through challenging times.
Wisdom	Good judgment and understanding of that which is true or good.
Worship	The act of honoring God in public or private.

World Church	The combination of all churches throughout the globe of our denomination. The many symbols of the cross.
Yes	The only answer to God's request.
Zion	The place we want to go; the city of God.

Epilogue "First"

Bishop
Darryl B. Starnes, Sr.
Senior Bishop of The
African Methodist Episcopal Zion Church

There is always only one first. There is always only one person whom God chooses to embrace the unique challenges, to endure the unique hardships, and to enjoy the unique opportunities of being the first. Eve will go down in history as the first woman, as the first wife, and as the first mother for the human race. The Prophetess Deborah will go down in history as the first woman to be a judge for Israel, God's chosen people. Mary Magdalene will go down in history as the first person, male or female, to witness to the resurrection of Christ. In the nearly two thousand years that have followed, many women have taken their places in the history of the world and in the history of the church as the first. Since the founding of The African Methodist Episcopal Zion Church in 1796, many women have made their marks, as leaders and as trailblazers, but it was not until 1896, that the Rev. Julia Foote became the first woman to be ordained a deacon, and not until 1898, that the Rev. Mary Small became the first woman to be ordained an elder. The

AME Zion Church would have to wait another one hundred and ten years for a woman to be elected a bishop. In 2008, the Right Rev. Mildred Bonnie Hines, a native of Mount Airy, North Carolina, became the first woman to be elected and consecrated to the episcopacy.

Bishop Hines took seriously her call to the ministry, both by preparing herself academically and by developing the spiritual gifts with which God had endowed her. Early in her ministry, she began to make a name for herself as a captivating teacher of God's word and as an electrifying preacher of Christ's gospel. Soon she was in great demand as a teacher and preacher, not only throughout the bounds of the Western North Carolina Conference, where she began her traveling ministry, but also throughout the country, and beyond. Her pastorates included the Saint Peters AME Zion Church in Gastonia, NC and the Walls Memorial AME Zion Church in Charlotte, NC. It was not long before she was not only pastoring churches with great success, but she was also becoming the featured speaker and/or presenter at connectional meetings, including Missionary Conventions, Christian Education Conventions, and Evangelism Congresses. Her anointed teaching and preaching had captured the imagination of the constituents of The African Methodist Episcopal Zion Church worldwide. After the 2004 General Conference, she was transferred to the Southwest Rocky Mountain Conference, which is a part of the Western Episcopal District, and was appointed the pastor of the

First AME Zion Church in Los Angeles, CA. It was from that pulpit that she was elected the 98th Bishop in the line of succession in The AME Zion Church at the 2008 General Conference in Atlanta, GA.

Bishop Hines' legacy as a bishop cannot be overstated. For four years, she served as the presiding bishop of the Western West African Episcopal District, which includes the Cote D'Ivoire, the East Ghana, the Mid-Ghana, the North Ghana, the West Ghana, the Liberia, and the Toga Annual Conferences. For four years, she served as the presiding bishop of the Southwestern Delta Episcopal District, which includes the Arkansas, the Louisiana, the Oklahoma, the South Mississippi, the Texas, and the West Tennessee-Mississippi Annual Conferences. For six years, she served as the presiding bishop of the South Atlantic Episcopal District, which includes the Georgia, the Palmetto, the Pee Dee, and the South Carolina Annual Conferences. She was the chairperson of the Clinton College Board of Trustees for six years. She represented the AME Zion Church on many ecumenical groups, such as the Pan-Methodist Commission and others, and chaired several administrative boards during her fourteen years as a bishop. Most importantly, she was the first woman to shatter the two hundred and twelve-year-old glass ceiling, letting the women of The African Methodist Episcopal Zion Church know that their gifts and their graces can also make room for them to be elevated to the high office of bishop in the church.

Photo Gallery

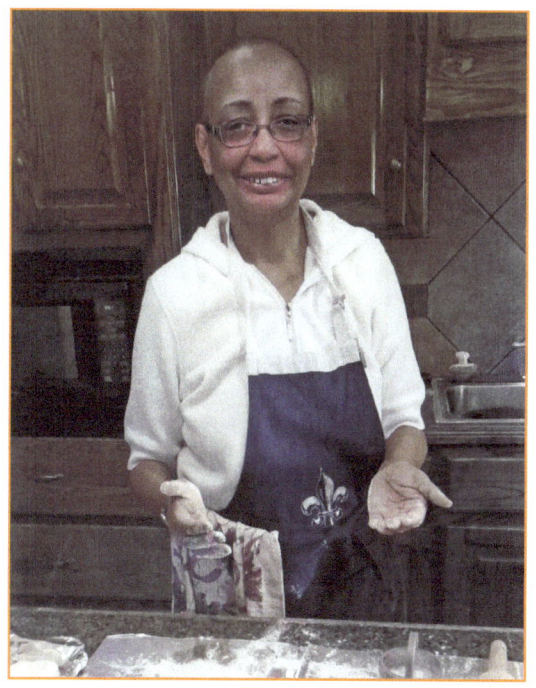

Group Hears Miss Hines

Mildred Hines is many things. Native of Mount Airy, college student, former department store employee, "big sister" to four teen-agers and daughter of proud parents.

In addition to the above, she is also St. Paul AME Church's very concerned and very respected YPD President, Sunday School Teacher, member of the Senior Choir, Bible student, Christian, and a very good speaker.

It is this young lady who challenged Missionaries of the Western District of the African Methodist Church (AME) to, first of all, find out what their real missions are, and secondly, to organize themselves to work toward those missions.

"Bonnie", as she is affectionately known to her relatives and friends, is

MILDRED HINES

Saturday, April 30, she spoke on the purposes of the Missionary Society and how they could be more successful if they were organized. She further stated that most Missionary Societies were not doing all that they were suppose to do. Speaking more forceful than usual, Bonnie challenged Missionaries to feed the hungry, visit the sick, help those families that are in need, and carry out other duties

Thank You

Thank You to the Board of Bishops who served as her colleagues and her mentors.

These 13 godly men became the big brothers she never had. Thank you, and . . .

To God Be the Glory!

www.ingramcontent.com/pod-product-compliance
Ingram Content Group UK Ltd.
Pitfield, Milton Keynes, MK11 3LW, UK
UKHW060124240426
12049UKWH00011B/151